IMAGES
of America
PICKERINGTON

In 1815, Abraham Pickering, seen here, purchased more than 80 acres of land in Violet Township from his father-in-law, James Looker. He wanted to establish a town, so after the land was cleared, he set aside a portion for a church, a school, and a cemetery. After Gen. Andrew Jackson defeated the British in New Orleans that year, Pickering named the new town Jacksonville in his honor. (Courtesy of Pickerington-Violet Township Historical Society.)

ON THE COVER: E.D. Kraner opened a mercantile store in 1872 at the corner of Columbus Street and Lockville Road in Pickerington. It offered a little bit of everything, including groceries, dry goods, and even a post office. (Courtesy of Pickerington-Violet Township Historical Society.)

IMAGES of America
PICKERINGTON

Christine A. Bryant on behalf of the
Pickerington-Violet Township Historical Society

Copyright © 2013 by Christine A. Bryant on behalf of the Pickerington-Violet Township Historical Society
ISBN 978-1-5316-5962-2

Published by Arcadia Publishing
Charleston, South Carolina

Library of Congress Control Number: 2012949831

For all general information, please contact Arcadia Publishing:
Telephone 843-853-2070
Fax 843-853-0044
E-mail sales@arcadiapublishing.com
For customer service and orders:
Toll-Free 1-888-313-2665

Visit us on the Internet at www.arcadiapublishing.com

*For my family, who have encouraged and
supported my growth as a writer*

CONTENTS

Acknowledgments		6
Introduction		7
1.	Violet Township and Early Pickerington	9
2.	Family Ties	25
3.	Agriculture and Business	37
4.	Schools	57
5.	Religious Freedom	79
6.	Clubs and Organizations	87
7.	Growth and Government	97
8.	Landmarks and Events	107
9.	Arts and People	119

ACKNOWLEDGMENTS

A project of this magnitude is not possible without the help of those who have a vested interest in preserving history so that future generations can learn and benefit from those who came before them.

A thank-you goes to Sandy Shalton, acquisitions editor at Arcadia Publishing, for her patience and guidance through the duration of this project. Thank you, as well, to the Pickerington-Violet Township Historical Society, which provided every photograph in this book—specifically Maggie Arendt, Joan Heft, Rita Ricketts, John Ricketts, Lois Williamson, Patsy Patrick Woodruff, and Gary Taylor, who researched public documents, archives, and other materials to ensure this book had the most accurate and complete information as possible.

A special thank-you goes to Peggy Portier, who tirelessly made herself available to answer questions, conduct research, and offer support. Lastly, thank you, to our families, for support during this project.

INTRODUCTION

From its early days up to the present, the citizens of Pickerington and Violet Township have taken pride in their community—their churches and schools, libraries and government buildings, and historic homes and businesses. In 1991, Ohio secretary of state Sherrod Brown certified Pickerington as a city, and at just more than 11 square miles, it is the second-largest city by area in Fairfield County.

Located just east of Columbus, Pickerington is a suburb and often attracts tourists who want to take a step back in time by perusing the small shops in Olde Pickerington Village. Yet one does not have to travel far outside the historic downtown area to find modern restaurants, stores, and sprawling neighborhoods. Beyond the city limits, Violet Township still features rolling hills, farmland, and prairies. But as the city continues to grow, the landscape is constantly changing.

One of the jewels found in downtown Pickerington is the Carnegie library, a historic landmark built in 1916 with a $10,000 grant from industrialist Andrew Carnegie. Carnegie provided the funds to community members so they could have a better-equipped building to serve as the Pickerington Public Library. When the library moved to its new location in 1993, the Pickerington-Violet Township Historical Society moved its museum into the Carnegie library building. The building, which is itself a treasure, now includes hundreds of smaller treasures.

The historical society has collected artifacts and photographs from the past 200 years. The museum features everything from the original town pump to antique household items, school furnishings, and birth and death certificates. There is even a collection of Pickerington-Violet Township High School graduating class photographs, dating from 1909 to 1981. There are also hundreds of photographs displayed throughout the museum, some of which are featured in this book.

Nearly 200 years ago, Abraham Pickering had a vision to create a town. To do so, he bought extra land from his father-in-law, James Looker, who had bought land at a public sale in 1811 in Violet Township, in the northwest corner of Fairfield County. The county was formally organized in 1800 as part of the Northwest Territory. The name of the township stemmed from the abundance of purple violets found in the area at the time.

Looker opted not to live on the land he had purchased, instead giving each of his children a piece. His daughter, Ann, and her husband, Abraham Pickering, built a log home along Sycamore Creek. Pickering hired surveyors to lay out his vision of a town, making sure to reserve space for a cemetery, a school, and a Methodist church. New townspeople began building log homes and businesses, but the town lacked one important feature—a name.

In 1815, Gen. Andrew Jackson defeated the British at the Battle of New Orleans, giving Pickering an idea. He rushed to the town's trading post, announcing that he had a name for the town. He explained the news of Jackson's victory and told the townspeople the new name of their town was Jacksonville, in honor of the "fighting son-of-a-gun, Old Hickory." Pickering's influence on the town left an impression on residents, and in 1827, they petitioned the state legislature to change the name of their town to instead honor Pickering for his service to his community. That year, the town's name was changed to Pickerington.

It is difficult to say whether Pickering could have imagined the growth Pickerington has experienced in these past 200 years. One thing is for certain, though; several people in Pickerington's history have made their marks on the city and helped make it the community it is today. Although it is impossible to name every person and organization that has played a significant role in the development of Pickerington and Violet Township, we hope this book gives a glimpse into the rich history of this community.

One
Violet Township and Early Pickerington

Some of the town's most important development occurred in its early years. In the mid-1860s, canal systems flourished in the eastern United States, and in Violet Township, people settled in the vicinity of the Ohio and Erie Canal. This allowed area farmers and businessmen to ship their products to other markets.

The railroads later replaced the canals, allowing faster transport of people and goods. By 1865, Pickerington had grown to have 150 residents and 37 buildings, with businesses including taverns, hotels, and general stores. A more centralized government began to form in the late 1800s, when community leaders constructed a "township house" with offices for government officials.

The first plat of Jacksonville was filed on September 15, 1815. In 1827, citizens honored Pickering by petitioning the state legislature to change the name of the town to Pickerington. The legislature approved the act the same year.

Between 1785 and 1900, the US Congress established grants of public lands to support education, transportation development, veterans' benefits, and new farm settlement from Ohio westward. Pres. James Madison awarded this land grant to Samuel Chaney on June 9, 1814, allowing him to acquire farmland in Violet Township's Section 32, which is now south of Little Walnut Creek on Waterloo South Road. This farm was then sold to Samuel Loucks in 1828, and acquired in 1838 by Jacob and Anna Brenner. Members of the Brenner family still farm this land today.

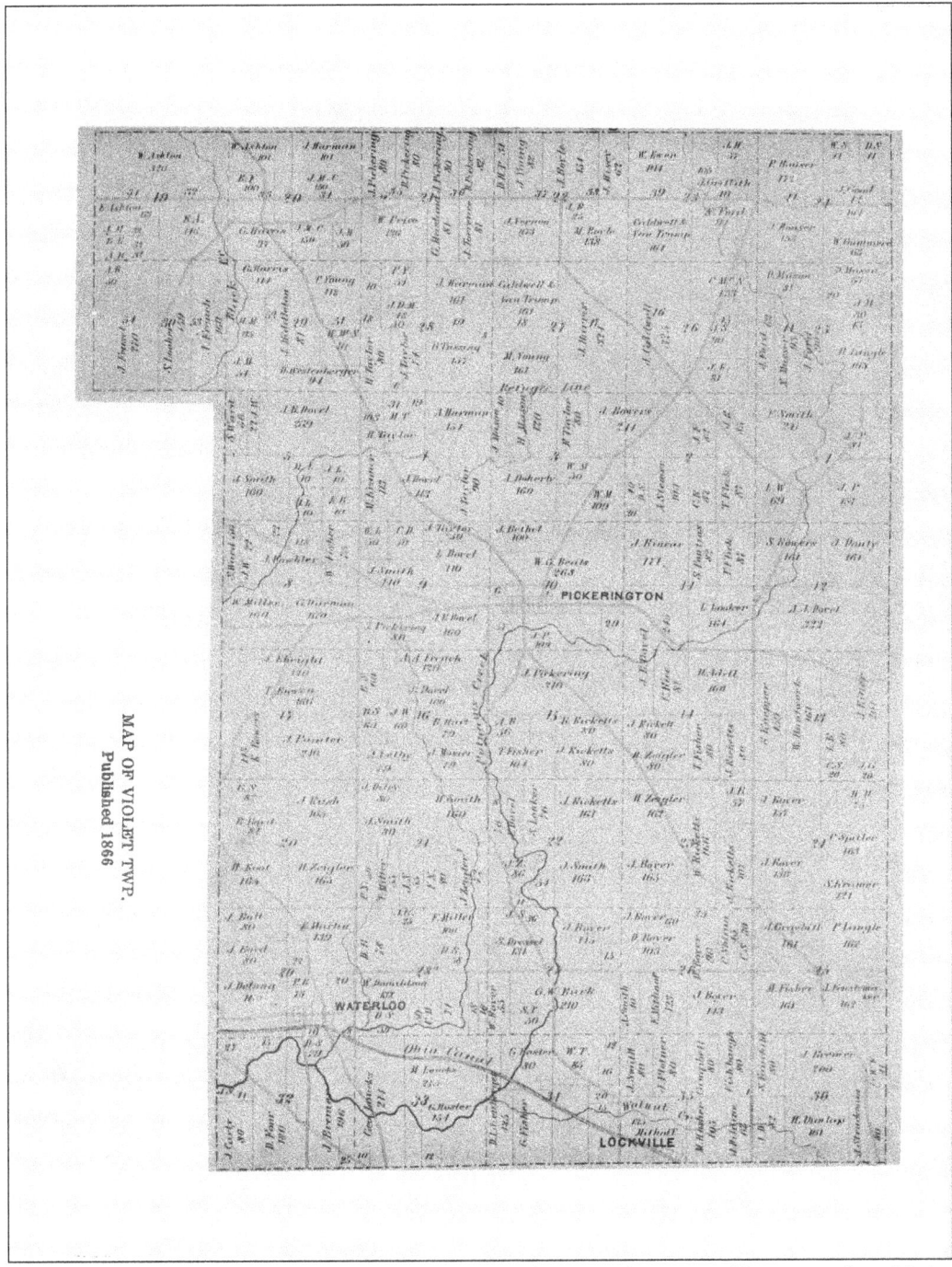

MAP OF VIOLET TWP.
Published 1866

A township is typically made up of 36 sections, each one mile square. However, when Violet Township was laid out in 1808, it was six miles wide and eight miles long. This was because a portion of it was a "refugee tract," in which free land was set aside for Canadian refugees who had aided colonists during the Revolutionary War. In 1851, the state legislature removed six sections of the territory, including the village of Canal Winchester, from Violet Township, and annexed them to Franklin County for political reasons.

Constructed in 1883, this two-story building was originally located at 15 East Columbus Street. It was moved to make room for the Carnegie library (building to the left), where the Pickerington-Violet Township Historical Society Museum is housed today. Known as the township house because it provided offices for the Violet Township trustees, it also housed Pickerington's village council. It was razed in the mid-1950s to make room for a new fire department building.

Along with several other watering holes, this 1880 tavern at the northeast corner of Columbus and Center Streets flourished during the construction of the railroad, which brought a growth spurt to Pickerington. The village did not see another major growth spurt until the construction of Interstate 70 in the late 1960s.

Constructed in 1888, this covered bridge spanned Sycamore Creek on Lockville Road, south of Columbus Street in Pickerington. It was replaced by an iron bridge in 1917. Standing at the left side of the bridge in this 1910 photograph is Kenneth W. Taylor. Most of the covered bridges in Fairfield County were built between 1871 and 1906. The first road in Violet Township opened in 1811, around where Amanda Northern Road is today. It carried supplies for soldiers fighting in the War of 1812. The next important road built in the township, between Somerset and Columbus, is now State Route 256.

Canals such as this one allowed area farmers and businessmen to ship their products to Southern markets. This photograph, taken in 1890, shows the remains of an Ohio and Erie Canal stonemasonry lock in Lockville. Canal systems flourished in this part of the country in the mid-1800s, and with the canals came development. In Violet Township, people settled their homes and businesses near the Ohio and Erie Canal in the Lockville-Waterloo area, in the southernmost area of Violet Township.

The Valley House, a popular hotel and tavern, is seen in this 1882 photograph at the northwest corner of Columbus and Center Streets. It also featured a livery stable in the rear. The building was constructed in 1865 as the Amos Breakbill Hotel. It burned to the ground in a historic 1927 fire that threatened to destroy the entire village.

This 1890 photograph shows the remains of the Mithoff Distillery. The Mithoff brothers built a store in the late 1840s in Lockville that served as a whiskey distillery, a saloon, a general store, and a post office. The distillery was one of the most successful components of the business and was one of the largest in this part of the country at the time. The Mithoffs used more than 300 bushels of corn every day to produce 1,200 gallons of whiskey. However, around 1870, the distillery portion of the business declined because of new federal taxes and the emergence of temperance organizations.

This late-1800s telephone was part of the old Woodpecker telephone line. Until 1991, the telephone hung in the home of Francis Leroy Millar in Violet Township, in the same room where it was originally installed by his great-grandfather Jacob Pickering. The Woodpecker line serviced 14 telephones and ran from Main Street in Wagram along Blacklick-Eastern and Milnor Roads to Pickerington.

Pickerington Tile Mill owner W.E. Fenstermaker can be seen at far right with unidentified employees in this early-1900s photograph. The tile mill was constructed in 1882 on the east side of Hill Road North near the railroad tracks in the village. The mill sold brick, tile, coal, lime, cement, and fertilizers. It discontinued its operations in 1931.

The railroads quickly replaced the canals as a means to transport people and goods. In 1879, Pickerington townspeople built a freight and passenger depot, and the Toledo & Ohio Central Railroad line through Pickerington was completed a year later. Each day, six passenger trains came through the depot (seen here in 1910), which was the social center of the community. The depot closed in 1958.

Six workers sit on a railroad cart after working on the Toledo & Ohio Central Railroad, which ran through Pickerington. This railroad section gang kept the track smooth and in running order. The Pickerington depot served as a communication and transportation connection to the outside world.

In this 1910 photograph, Dr. W.B. Taylor (right), his wife, Nellie Blanche (center), and Nellie Pugh enjoy some recreational fishing at the state dam on the Ohio and Erie Canal, between Lockville and Waterloo in southern Violet Township. Dr. Taylor's son, Kenneth, continued the practice of medicine in Pickerington, from 1930, when he joined his father, until his retirement in 1976.

Ida Fenstermaker poses in front of her house at 63 West Church Street in Pickerington. She was the sister of William Fenstermaker, who started the village's tile mill. Ida often took in boarders here, and the 1910 census shows that William also owned a house. William and his wife, Hattie, had several kids, including a boy named Frank. It is possible that Frank and his family at one time lived with Ida, according to the 1915 Fairfield County farmer's directory.

Pickerington citizens and a telephone crew install telephones on North Center Street in 1905. The railroad depot is in the background. The old Woodpecker telephone line, also known as the "short line," served Violet Township from the late 1800s through the early 1900s. It came south from Wagram to Jacob Pickering's home and went on to the James C. Belt home on Church Street, across from the Pickerington Creamery.

In the foreground of this early-1900s photograph is the retirement home of Billy and Eleanor Hoy, which still stands at 60 East Columbus Street. Billy was a Civil War veteran who farmed land in the area of Saylor-Stemen Road. This photograph was taken by A.M. "Gus" Alexander, who took most of the early photographs in the area.

In this 1910 photograph, George Motts and William J. Milnor are moving their grocery and meat market. They had operated this business at 14 East Columbus Street for five years. Henry Tschopp operated a general store here during the 1880s and 1890s. When the frame building was destroyed by fire in 1924, Brooks Huntwork constructed a new building, which served as a restaurant operated by Huntwork for a few years, followed by Clarence England and then Walter and Wilma Moore until 1956. The new building currently houses Solomon's Carpet.

Jacob Dovel (right) and his wife, Elizabeth, came from Virginia to Violet Township in the early 1820s and purchased a 320-acre tract of land east of Pickerington, part of an area that now includes the Shadow Oaks, Simsbury, and Pickerington Hills subdivisions. Dovel gave a house and 160 acres to each of his five children after each married. The barnyard on their son Frank's property is pictured (above) in the early 1900s. While Frank Dovel's brick house still stands at 50 Hill Road South, his barn was destroyed in 1967.

Each year, the train from Columbus arrived in Pickerington for the annual Homecoming and Labor Day celebration. Here, in the early 1900s, townspeople gather to watch the train's arrival and to greet passengers.

Two
Family Ties

Today's Pickerington looks very different than the dirt roads and sprawling fields of 200 years ago. The busy residential and business community has experienced great growth, and current citizens can thank many of the founding families that laid the groundwork for potential development in the future.

Among the most notable families are the Kraners, who operated a general store in Pickerington and were associated with the Pickerington Bank. The patriarch of the family, Michael Kraner, emigrated from Germany to Baltimore, Maryland, in the mid-1700s and served in the Revolutionary War. He had two sons, Henry and John Michael. Many of the Kraner descendents played crucial roles in the development of Pickerington. Both Henry's son, William H., and his grandson, E.D. Kraner, operated general stores in town.

Another notable family was the Dovels. The 160 acres given to Frank Dovel by his father, Jacob, have been very important to the community, as the present Pickerington High School Central athletic stadium, Ridgeview Junior High School, and the city's sewage treatment plant sit on part of that land. Frank also served as grand marshal in many homecoming parades and was an avid booster of Pickerington.

One cannot mention Pickerington families without mentioning the Pickerings, who founded the town. Several other citizens have left their mark as well, including Cleo Mason Richter, who took over as postmistress after the death of her father, Phillip B. Mason, and who, throughout her life, recorded local events happening in town. There are also the Taylors, who practiced medicine in Pickerington for 75 years and were instrumental in building some of the city's most popular parks.

Mary Ann Price Pickering (standing, far left) was born in Maryland on December 2, 1822, and was the wife of David Harrison Pickering, who moved to Pickerington from Virginia. Their son, Jacob (standing, second from left) was born on February 25, 1845, and was the great-nephew of town founder Abraham Pickering. This photograph features four generations of Pickerings. Standing next to Jacob is his son, Otha Allen Pickering, and seated, from left to right, are Jacob's wife, Lavinnia Allen Pickering; Otha's wife, Mary Maxwell Pickering; and Otha and Mary's baby daughter, Agnes Lavinnia Pickering.

Hazel Bish Cook (left) and Bernice Bish Bickel stand at the grave of their great-great-grandfather Abraham Pickering in Violet Cemetery in 1965. He was the founder of Pickerington.

The Kraner family moved from Baltimore, Maryland, in 1805 and settled in what was later called Violet Township. Michael Kraner, seen here, was 16 when he traveled by wagon to his new home. A year later, Pres. Thomas Jefferson finally signed the land patent granting Michael's father, Henry Kraner, and his uncle John Michael Kraner 640 acres southeast of what is now Pickerington. Michael married Nancy Nolan in 1825 and they had 12 children. He died at age 83.

E.D. Kraner (far right), the son of William H. Kraner and nephew of Michael Kraner, opened his own mercantile store in 1872 in Pickerington. That year, he also began serving as postmaster, a position he held for more than 25 years. He and his wife, Ella (far left), had four children—Charles, James, Maud, and William H. (not pictured). The eldest son, Charles (standing next to his father), graduated from Ohio Northern University with a degree in pharmacy and then completed a doctor of medicine in 1905. He later became ill with a serious ear infection and lost hearing in both his ears, making it impossible to continue his medical practice. He then returned to Pickerington to operate the Kraner store. Charles Kraner died in 1941 and is buried in Violet Cemetery.

James Garfield Kraner was active in Violet Township affairs and was part of the committee that brought Pickerington a Carnegie library. In 1908, he went to New York City to meet with a committee of the Carnegie Library Commission. The second child of E.D. Kraner, he also served on the Violet Township Board of Education from 1934 to 1942, taught at several rural schools, and was a member of the original board of directors at the Pickerington Bank. He married Isabel Clem in 1918 and they had two children, Mary Ellen and James Clem Kraner. James and Isabel are buried in Violet Cemetery.

Frank Dovel, seen in both these images, acted as grand marshal in several homecoming parades and was an enthusiastic booster of Pickerington in the late 1800s and early 1900s. He also owned and maintained a racetrack, where Ridgeview Junior High School is today, 130 Hill Road South. Dovel was the son of Jacob and Elizabeth Dovel, who moved from Virginia to Violet Township in the early 1820s. Frank's brick house still stands at 50 Hill Road South.

This c. 1906 family portrait shows Nicholas and Anna Elizabeth Fishbaugh and their nine daughters. They are, from left to right, (first row) Bertha, Rachel, and Thursie; (second row) Georgia and Annie Elizabeth (being held by their parents); and (third row) Christina, Florence, Maude, and Mary Jane.

Arthur J. Good came to Pickerington in 1913 and eventually took over ownership of the local creamery. He then formed Pickerington Creamery, Inc. and developed it into a modern, full-scale operation. The company's headquarters remained in Pickerington until the business closed in 1972.

In 1901, Grace Bowen, daughter of Irven and Florence "Florida" Dovel Bowen, married Orin C. Belt, the son of James Belt, who operated the first flour mill in Pickerington. The family farm where the wedding was held was named Graceland and located on the southwest corner of State Route 256 and Refugee Road. Graceland was home to a nationally recognized herd of Guernsey milk cows.

Mr. and Mrs. Benoni Stemen sit in their rocking chairs on September 6, 1906. The Stemens, whose families came from Pennsylvania, were Mennonites and had a farm on the northeast corner of Wright and Diley Roads. In the 1890s, Stemen deeded a plot of land to the small Mennonite congregation to build a church. That small church building, now painted red and used for farm storage, is owned by the C.M. Raab heirs and located at 280 Diley Road on the west side of Pickerington.

Cleo Mason Richter was born in Pickerington on December 4, 1907, at the Columbus Street home of her parents, Jennie M. and Philip B. Mason. Cleo attended Pickerington High School and was the valedictorian of the class of 1925. She graduated from Ohio State University with a degree in education and taught at Pickerington High School for seven years. Her father was the postmaster, and she worked as a post office clerk under his supervision. She married Raye F. Richter in 1938, and after her father's death in 1940, she became Pickerington's postmistress, serving until 1967. Cleo lived her entire life on the same street and was an interested, faithful witness and recorder of local events and happenings.

Virgil Diley was a lifelong resident of Violet Township, graduating from Pickerington High School and Ohio State University. After serving in World War II, he was a high school teacher and a rural mail carrier before replacing Cleo Mason Richter as postmaster in 1967. He was also president of the Rural Letter Carriers Association of Fairfield County.

Dr. Kenneth Taylor began practicing medicine in Pickerington with his father, Dr. W.B. Taylor, in 1930. When Kenneth retired in 1976, it ended 75 years—73 of which were continuous—of Taylor doctors in Pickerington.

In this 1980 photograph, brothers Kenneth (left) and Emerson Taylor shake hands at the new tennis courts in Sycamore Creek Park. These were named in their honor after they, like their father, Dr. W.B. Taylor, donated land for public park space. In 1941, the elder Taylor and A.J. Good had acquired property across from the Grange Hall on Lockville Road that they donated to Pickerington. It was later named Victory Park.

Sarah England is seen here with her grandchildren, from left to right, Raymond, Elizabeth, and Paul, in 1907 or 1908. The children's parents were Homer and Angie Poff England. Sarah was born in June 1832 in Pennsylvania and died in Pickerington on May 12, 1914. She married Peter England, a farmer, and had the first of her 15 children at age 17. Elizabeth, the infant in this photograph, was the Pickerington homecoming queen in 1920.

Richard Ashton married Betty Mary Bish in 1906, around the time this photograph was taken. Ashton's father, Joseph, and uncle Edward purchased more than 500 acres in northwest Violet Township in 1818. Richard and Betty's farm included 200 acres that later became part of Blacklick Woods Metro Park in Reynoldsburg. Other parts of the Ashtons' property now include the Interstate 70 and Route 256 interchange, Wesley Ridge Retirement Community, and Taylor Square Shopping Center. Richard died at age 83 in 1957, and Betty died in 1961.

Three
AGRICULTURE AND BUSINESS

Before the railroad came to town in 1880, small businesses, quaint houses, and rolling farm fields dominated the landscape. But when the Toledo & Central Ohio Railroad arrived, it brought immigrants, more development, and a new market for farmers' produce and livestock.

That year, construction on the Pickerington Mill began after William and Joseph Strickler bought three lots from Jesse and Adaline Hager. Work on the mill was completed by 1883, and ownership of the mill changed a number of times over the years, as did the manufacturing process it used. As times and needs changed, it went from using stone burrs to new steel rolls in 1896. In 1911, mill operators changed the power that operated the machinery from steam to a natural gas engine. The mill was first used to produce flour, but operations later expanded to include grain and feed.

The Pickerington Creamery was another major business that had a significant impact on the community. It began in 1900 after a small group of local farmers organized a local neighborhood creamery called the Elgin Butter Company. Arthur J. Good eventually acquired ownership of the company and began buying several other small creameries in central Ohio. As roads and transportation improved, so did the company's fleet of trucks. Good added three 1,200-pound churns and copyrighted the Mayflower brand the creamery produced. In addition to butter, the creamery added eggs, poultry, dried buttermilk, cheese, and nonfat dry milk. Before Good's death in 1960, he successfully grew the company to epic proportions, using state-of-the-art equipment, some of which were the first of their kind in the United States. He also left a lasting impact on manufacturing operations and food distribution, and set a model for how to successfully grow a business.

While the Pickerington Mill and the Pickerington Creamery were responsible for much of the manufacturing growth in the community, the town's heart and soul rested in the small businesses that dotted the streets. Grocery store operators took great pride in offering their customers the freshest produce, with some driving to Columbus each day to buy freshly picked vegetables and fruits. In addition to selling food and other necessities, they also offered post office services and a place for local organizations to gather.

In the late 1800s and early 1900s, taverns and hotels flourished in Pickerington, as did specialty shops like Jesse Hager's shoe shop, Adolph Schultz's jewelry store, and S.S. Good's Harness Shop, which repaired much of the gear horse teams used to drag logs to mills in town. Most of the outlying area was still made up of farmland. Graceland Farm, for example, was at the corner of Route 256 and Refugee Road, which is now a major intersection in Pickerington.

Graceland Farm, owned by O.C. Belt and his wife, Grace Dovel Bowen Belt, was at the corner of Route 256 and Refugee Road, now the site of several retail sites. The main farmhouse was one of five houses built by Jacob B. Dovel for his children. At one time, the family owned all four corners of the now-popular intersection.

This is one of the many barns on Graceland Farm where cows, always of the Guernsey breed, were milked by milking machines—the forerunner of modern dairy facilities—where cows were fastened in stanchions and milked as they stood there.

Everett Hively (right) and Paul Priddy load bulk milk cans into a Wetherell Dairy truck. Dairy farms were one of the many agricultural businesses in Fairfield County in the early 1900s.

After the railroad came to Pickerington in 1880, construction on the Pickerington Mill began. It was completed by 1883 and was largely operated by the Wooley family. Located along the railroad tracks at the northwest corner of Church and Center Streets, it was a large operation where farmers came to ship their grain and buy feed. H.R. Wooley first operated it as a flour mill, but later, H.H. Wooley expanded the mill's operations to include grain and feed. It closed in 1971.

James "Daddy" Belt was one of the original owners of the Pickerington Mill, before selling it to the Wooley family in 1906. Here, Belt holds the bridle of his horse, which is attached to a carriage. In addition to being a successful businessman and mayor, Belt was also known for his impressive beard, which at one point reached all the way to his knees.

In 1900, a small group of local farmers organized and started a local neighborhood creamery, the Elgin Butter Company. In 1913, Arthur J. Good arrived in Pickerington by train and showed interest in the butter company. About six months later, Creighton Pearce sold one-half interest to Good, and the company operated under the name Pearce and Good. When Pearce retired, Good acquired full ownership of the creamery. This sole ownership continued until 1935, when it was incorporated into Pickerington Creamery, Inc. Good died in 1960 after leading the company for 45 years.

The creamery's employees in 1928 include, from left to right, (first row) Andrew Burnard, Earl Smoke, unidentified, Raymond Congrove, "Bus" Smoke, Francis Burnard, Bill Sparks, Clyde Carpenter, Loren Hawbecker, and Roy Camp; (second row) Clair Weaver, William Spears, Roy Potter, Todd Ricketts, unidentified, Nelson Whitehed, Milt E. Gardner, unidentified, Frank Clark, Val Houser, unidentified, and Raymer Anderson; (third row) Byron Grable, Paul Houser, Cora Fenstermaker, Marjory (Blauser) Blackstone, Helen (Fenstermaker) Spears, Everett Tharp, owner Arthur J. Good, Mildred (Sallee) Taylor, Gladys (Nicodemus) Bundy, Maude Kraner, Dan Fishbaugh, Wilfred Brenneman, George McVeigh, and Jim Brenneman.

In 1921, the Pickerington Creamery plant burned to the ground. In approximately six months, workers built a completely new facility that included modern upgrades and technology. Just a few years later, in the mid-to-late-1920s, owner Arthur J. Good acquired the old West Jefferson Creamery and several other smaller plants. Throughout the years, equipment was replaced with more updated production machinery.

This 1973 photograph shows the Pickerington Creamery cheese and egg barn on West Borland Street. In the early 1970s, the creamery purchased the Central Ohio Distributing Company in Reynoldsburg. Soon after, in 1972, the Pickerington Creamery's butter and dry milk business was sold to Beatrice Foods Company, which consolidated its manufacturing operations with its other plant in Columbus.

Edward F. Brooke, seen here in 1925, and his father, Linden J. Brooke, were lumber dealers and most likely supplied the materials for this wooden oil derrick. Violet Township's first oil well was drilled in 1919 on the Andrew Stemen farm, on the north side of Wright Road at the intersection of Schoolhouse Road.

Harry Houck Hanna was born and raised on Columbus Street in a house built by his grandfather William Houck, which was later torn down to make room for the parking lot of the Pickerington Bank. After serving in World War I, Hanna married and purchased a house in 1922. The next year, he built a garage next to the house and opened his own car repair business. The garage was built with bricks from the old tile mill that had been next to the railroad tracks along Route 256. Hanna's Auto Repair also served as the village's gas station, and the garage hosted local wrestling matches. Hanna eventually expanded his business and became one of the nation's first 300 Chrysler/Plymouth dealerships. In the 1960s, he sold the business and retired.

In the late 1800s and early 1900s, taverns and hotels flourished in Pickerington. Here, around 1900, a group congregates in front of the American Hotel. Among those on the porch are Annie Myers Grubb and Mary Kull Snoke, owner and operator of the hotel.

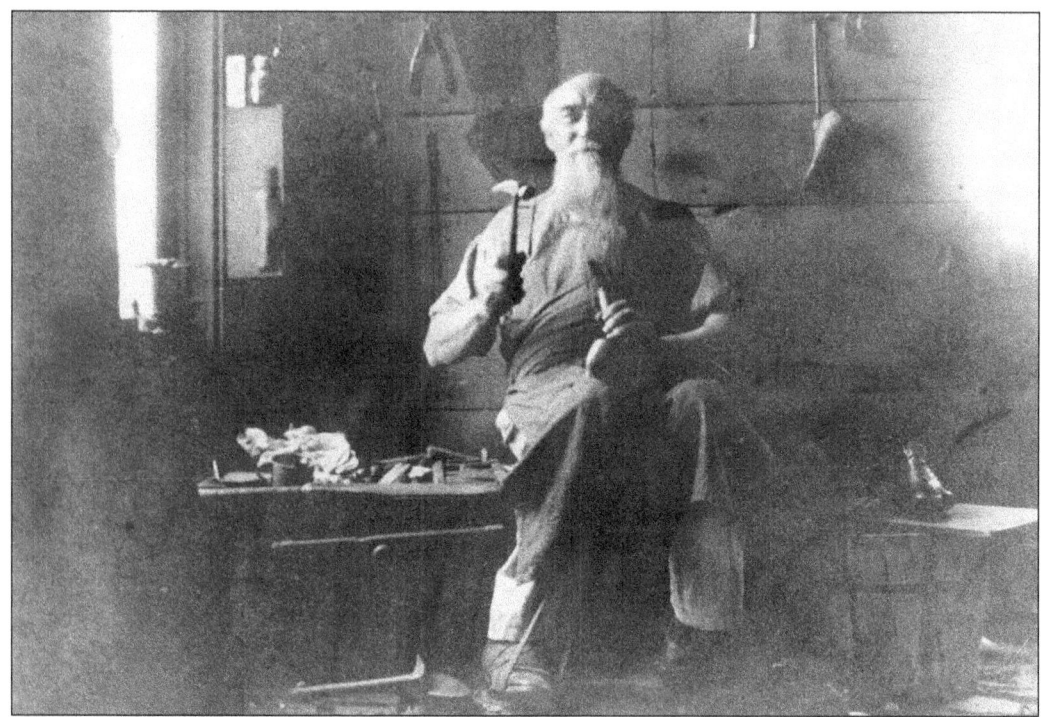

Jesse Hager operated a shoe shop in the early 1900s in Pickerington. He is seen here in 1908 holding the tools of his trade. Hager also served as the mayor and postmaster of Pickerington. He married Adaline Kraner, sister of general store owner E.D. Kraner. The Hagers had no children, but raised a boy named Hazlet Petty.

S.S. Good purchased a shop on West Columbus Street in the early 1900s where he taught the trade of harness-making to his sons, Mervin and Carlton. Good made and repaired much of the gear used by horse teams to drag logs to the mills in town to be processed.

E.D. Kraner's general store, seen here in the early 1900s, offered a little bit of everything, including groceries, dry goods like clothing and yard items, and even a post office. The building's second floor operated as a duckpin bowling alley with four lanes. The building later became a drugstore run by the Stiverson family and later by Bill Simon, who had the second floor remodeled as an apartment for him and his family.

Before opening, the Kraners distributed this sign advertising fresh goods and other items at their general store. Painted on the north side of the building in bold letter was Kraner's business motto: "The Best Possible Goods for the Least Possible Cash."

This address has been home to several businesses, but one of the first was Cyrus Smith's general store. Seen here in 1891, Smith (center, standing on steps) kept a variety of grocery items and goods for customers. He used the upstairs as his living quarters. Later, the store became the Fowler and Fancher general store, and in the early 1920s, it was purchased by Burch and Alma Newlon.

Adolph Schultz operated a jewelry store next to his home in the early 1900s. His wife, Caroline, stands in the center of this photograph, taken around the time the business opened. Schultz died in 1912 and the jewelry shop was moved.

Bill Moore operated Moore's grocery and meat market in the early 1900s. Seen here in the store in 1927 are, from left to right, Bill Moore, Clifford Moore, and Clarence England. At the time of the photograph, the Independent Order of Odd Fellows lodge was on the second floor. After the meat market closed, the store room on the first floor was rented by Elza "Ducky" Weaver for a meat and grocery store. The building once stood in the now-empty lot between 18 and 26 East Columbus Street.

Seen in this interior view of the Clover Farm Store are owner Frank Fenstermaker and his son Norman. The building, at 19 West Columbus Street, was constructed in 1885 by James Schirm, who operated a pharmacy there until 1934. Fenstermaker made weekly trips to Columbus to buy fresh produce for the store. On one of his trips, he was in an accident that left him in a coma until his death. After the accident, his son Bill took over the business and operated it until the 1960s.

Caldwell's grocery, at 18 East Columbus Street, was built by Daniel Petty in 1880. In 1909, William Caldwell acquired the property and opened a grocery store. He is seen here the year before he bought it. In 1928, Caldwell sold the building to Harry and Helen Ruse, who continued in the grocery business as a Red & White store. Helen Ruse was a schoolteacher, while Harry kept the store stocked with groceries. In the 1950s, Harry suffered a fatal heart attack while working in the store. The building became a billiard parlor in 1956 and has been home to a variety of businesses since.

Approximately 250 area farm families who were members of Violet Grange built a new hall at 36 Lockville Road and held their first meeting there on February 22, 1954. Violet Grange was initially formed in 1914 by 35 Violet Township farm families to serve as a "friend of the farmer." The group quickly evolved into being the social center of the community by organizing dinners, events, and charitable projects. Its building and property were sold to Violet Township in 2011.

A group of villagers sits outside of C.O. Beals's law office at 13 West Columbus Street in the early 1900s. In addition to his thriving law practice, Beals developed a lake and summer cottage community off East Street known as Beals Lake subdivision. Like several wooden structures around Pickerington, Beals's tiny law office building was moved. In the 1960s, the structure was sold to the Pickerington Board of Education for $1, and Dick Huntwork & Sons moved it for the second time to the southeast corner of the school athletic field, where it was used to store athletic equipment. It still stands along Sycamore Creek's bike path near Victory Park.

These men haul logs to a local hoop mill on Old Village Lot 97 on East Church Street in 1900. The hoop mill made wooden-barrel hoops from elm wood. When there were no more elm trees available, the mill left Pickerington and moved elsewhere. That mill was torn down by 1937.

East Columbus Street is seen here in the late 1940s. On the far left is Roy Huntwork's Mobil station, which was built in 1946. To the right of the gas station is the home of Jay Kocher and his family, where Kocher ran a barbershop. The next building to the right is Moore's Restaurant. Walter "Butch" and Wilma Moore operated the restaurant in the upstairs of the building and a pool hall in the basement. In 1957, the Moores sold their restaurant and soon after opened a new pool room in the building next door to the right. The tallest structure seen on the far right was built by the Independent Order of Odds Fellows in 1880 and was razed about 1947. The lot remains vacant. Note the head-in parking once used along Columbus Street.

In 1950, Garland Patrick and his father-in-law, Charles Exline, sold meats and groceries from this store located at 21 North Center Street. Isaly's Coffee Shop shared the lower level, while the upstairs served as a meeting place for the Grange, Boy Scouts, and Independent Order of Odd Fellows. The building had been constructed in 1929. On Saturday evenings during the 1940s, local residents were entertained with wrestling matches and movies held in the empty lot on the south side of the building.

In 1946, Raymond O. Williamson signed a lease with Frank Bish to operate the service station at 192 West Columbus Street in Pickerington. At the time, gas was 15¢ per gallon, bottled soda was 5¢, and tires sold for $9.95. The station's telephone number was FR7-4375. In 1953, Frank and Viola Bish sold the station to Williamson, and it was replaced with a new building in 1958. From its beginnings until the national gasoline shortage in 1973, the service station was open for business from 6:00 a.m. to 9:00 p.m., seven days a week. It closed in 2004.

Henry Blauser (right) claimed to be the first depositor in the Pickerington Bank in 1910 and the first depositor after a new bank was built in 1962 at 35 West Columbus Street in the village. He is seen here with Goff Courtright. The bank began operations with $25,000 and 62 stockholders. James G. Kraner served as the first cashier and the bank's sole employee for the first 15 years. He resigned in 1944 after 35 years. In 1976, the Pickerington Bank merged with Huntington National Bank.

This photograph shows the outside of the Pickerington Bank after it was robbed in the late 1950s. Both female tellers onsite said they refused to surrender the money. The robber then forced them into a back room and took $13,000. Yet a deposit of $6,000 from the creamery, left lying on the counter, was not taken. Police never caught the robber.

Four
SCHOOLS

Residents have taken pride in their schools for nearly two centuries, and Pickerington's schools are often the reason newcomers choose to live in the area. At one time, Violet Township had 19 either one- or two-room schoolhouses spread out across the township. The first school documented in Pickerington was in 1812, when a log building north of where the original Peace United Church stood on Cross Street was used as a school. Researchers believe it may have been used for church on Sundays as well.

In the late 1800s and early 1900s, Pickerington's schools were spread throughout Violet Township and known as country schools. A law in 1904, however, forced the district to completely reorganize and centralize the schools under a civil township organization that was administered through county officials. In 1905, the first Violet Township High School was organized, and construction began in 1907. The six-room building cost $15,000 to construct and was the first centralized school in the county. The class of 1909 was the first to graduate. Today, there are more than 10,000 students in the district, spread out over 14 modern facilities, making it the 18th-largest school district in the state.

Built in 1883 on East Street, the two-story Pickerington School seen in both images was known in Pickerington as the "school on the hill." In 1907, it was demolished to make way for Violet Township's consolidated grade and high school. On the left in the above image is the Knepper family home, which was destroyed in 1981.

Ricketts School No. 7 was built in the late 1890s near the corner of Pickerington and Busey Roads. Seen here in front of the school are, from left to right and identified by their later married names if known, (first row) J.C. Ziegler-Detwiler, Emma Mosier-Bish, Lillian Finney Root, Effie Finney, Frank Finney, Frank Hart, Vernon Ziegler, Lydia Mosier, Hugh Morath, Cora Mosier-Smith-Exline, Carrie Smith Ricker, Blanche Smith Klein, and Docia Fisher Holder; (second row) Minnie Hart, Emmer Ziegler, Cora Ziegler Benson, Barney Hart, Clem Ricketts, Walter Boyer, and Ethel Fisher Bish. There are also several children peeking out of the windows. Teacher O.H. Mosier is at far right.

The Fishbaugh School, also known as the Fishpaw School, was one of the first schools in Violet Township. It was at the corner of Allen and Basil Western Roads. Here, teachers and students pose in front of the school. On August 18, 1834, Jacob and Mary Grawl presented this small tract of land to the district's directors to be used for a school. The school then cost $1,250 to build.

Teacher Samual Raver (second row, center) poses with a group of his students at the one-room Peru School in 1899. The school was on Stemen Road, about one mile southeast of the Oregon School, which was located on Pickerington Road North midway between Stemen and Refugee Roads.

Pickerington School teacher Charles Kistler (second row, far left) and his 24 students pose for a school photograph in 1899. Today, there are two high schools in Pickerington—and more than 3,300 high school students enrolled.

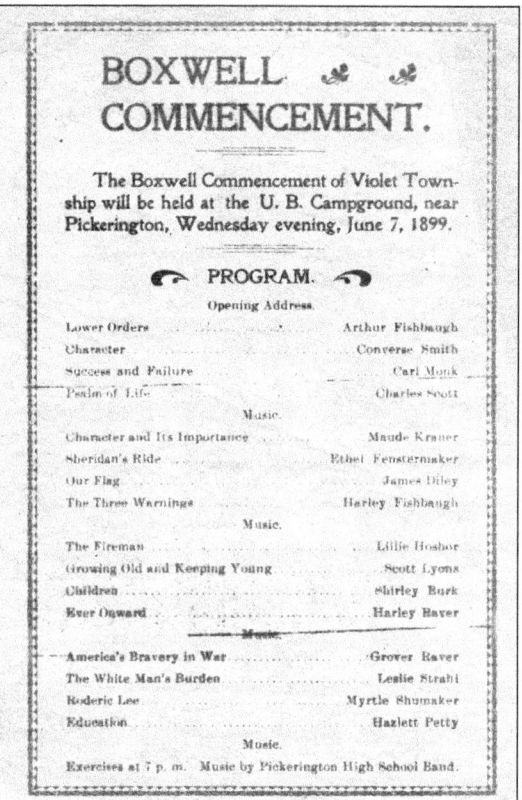

The quality of the schools in Ohio came into doubt in the late 1800s because the Ohio General Assembly was concerned about primary-level district schools in rural communities. In response, a new law in 1877 made school attendance compulsory. Later, the Boxwell exam was offered to eighth-grade graduates where high schools were not available to ensure that they had mastered the necessary components of their education. Passing students could then attend any high school in the county. The program at left is from a commencement held after the test on June 7, 1899, at the United Brethren campground (now the Tabernacle), just south of the city limits on Pickerington Road.

Alvin Ricketts was a schoolteacher who lived on Main Street (now Columbus Street) and taught in the one-room, log cabin Pickerington School located where the Carnegie library was later built at 15 East Columbus Street. He was born on January 20, 1839, to Chaney and Phoebe Ann Ricketts. He attended Pleasantville Academy, where students rode a wagon to school on Monday and stayed through the week. He was taught by Joseph Feman. Ricketts died on October 28, 1927.

Noah Moore and his dog Carlo pose for this photograph beside a school wagon. These wagons were used from 1907 into the 1920s to bring kids from outside town to the new consolidated school. This wagon appears to be one of the newer models at the time, with windows and an exhaust pipe for a heater. The Pickerington-Violet Township Historical Society features a small portable heater that would have been used at the time to heat the wagons. It is an enclosed metal can in which hot coals from the driver's home fire were placed. Some drivers also used bricks that were warmed by the fire and then laid on the floor of the wagon.

Mingo School was built in 1872 and operated until schools were centralized in 1907. It was on Diley Road on the north bank of Georges Creek. An earlier Mingo School on Diley Road closed the same year this one opened. Seen here are, from left to right, (first row) Minnie Fisher, Mabel Lunn, Ralph Patrick, Alice Fisher England, and Clara Boyer; (second row) Goff Courtright, Jess Weaver, Lester Stemen, Ralph Lunn, Zora Boyer, and unidentified; (third row) Mabel Patrick, Roxie McDaniel, Forest Weaver, Grover Young, Harry Boyer, and Harry Weaver; (fourth row) Homer Fisher, Harry Ricketts, Harold French, Homer French, two unidentified girls, and Mary Patrick. The school's teacher, Albert Black, is behind the students on the right side.

In 1907, the Pickerington School, known locally as the "school on the hill," was demolished to make way for Violet Township's consolidated grade and high school. Some of the men building the new school are Dave Cochenour (with the wheelbarrow), Ben Cochenour (sitting on the pile of bricks), Charles Shimp (on the wagon, left) and Rue Fishbaugh (on the wagon, right). The contractor listed was C.W. Ricket of Bremen, Ohio, who completed the project at a cost of $18,000.

In 1907, the Pickerington School District consolidated all of its country schools into one centralized school. At the time of centralization, the Pickerington School Board included, from left to right, (first row) John Talbot, principal and longtime teacher; and William Ackers, superintendent; (back row) John Peters; A.M. "Gus" Alexander, who took most of the early photographs of Pickerington; Allen Courtright; and W.W. Milnor.

Students and teachers begin the school year in their new consolidated building in 1907. The structure, on East Street, now houses the district offices.

Pictured in the science laboratory of the new Violet Township High School are, from left to right, Tom Kraner, teacher John Talbot, Rue Fishbaugh, Amy Lyons (Humphrey), Frank Fenstermaker, Perley C. Milnor, and Guy Fishbaugh. At the time, this was a very modern science lab.

The entire student body and the teachers of Violet Township High School pose for this photograph in 1908, the school's second year of operation. Before this school opened, students who finished eighth grade had to travel outside the township to go to high school. The teachers standing on the ground by the staircase are, from left to right, John Talbot, William Ackers (superintendent), Samuel Raver, Gussie Stemen, Eura L. Tussing, Elsie Tway (or Dorcas Truckmiller), Alice Hizey, and Blanche Lehman.

At the top of the roof in the center, John W. Blauser stands near where a school bell will be placed during the construction of the new school in 1907.

Violet Township High School housed all grades, from elementary school students through high school. Until 1915, the township library was on the top floor.

The class of 1909, the first graduating class of the new Violet Township High School, had only four students. They are, from left to right, (first row) Perley C. Milnor and Guy Fishbaugh; (second row) Amy G. Lyons and Rue Fishbaugh.

Aaron Boyer drove this typical school wagon for the 1907 Violet Township School. During the winter, curtains were rolled down to help keep the children warm and keep out the cold. The wagons had long benches on each side and were heated either with carbon sticks, brick foot warmers, or coal stoves. The district used the wagons until the 1920s.

Members of Violet Township High School's first basketball teams are seen here at Liberty Union during the first Fairfield County basketball tournament. The teams include, from left to right, (first row) Mary Hempy, Dorothea Kraner, Kate Keller, "Cap" Hoover, Lura Lane, Albert Turley, Mary B. Kraner, Dorothy Boyer, and Evelyn Myers; (second row) Kenneth Taylor, Roy Nicodemus, Edward Brooke, Raymond Boyer, Ralph England, and Carl Pinkerman. Pickerington did not have a football team until the 1970s.

Burke School was the last country school to enter the Violet Township High School system. It was at the northeast corner of Amanda Northern Road and Route 33. Teacher Grace Wagner is seen here with her students in 1922.

The 1935 Pickerington High School boys' basketball team photograph includes, from left to right, (first row) Theodore Manson, Lloyd Weaver, Harold Strahm, and Victor Smith; (second row) Harold Mauger, Grover Looker, Wayne Johnson, William Detwiler, Howard Tharp, and Ralph Smurr; (third row) William Henry Diley, Harry Gardner, manager Clearence Tharp, coach Raye F. Richter, John Derr, Gerold Reaver, and assistant manager Jack Beals.

The Pickerington High School boys' basketball team is seen here in 1936 on its way to Columbus to play Columbus Academy. Pictured are, from left to right, Harold Mauger, Ralph Smurr, Darl Walton, Lloyd Weaver, Wayne Johnson, Dolphus Walton, Herbert Vandemark, Lyle Huntwork, Kenneth Milnor, William Henry Diley, Edward Underwood, and coach Raye F. Richter.

The 25th reunion of the class of 1935 met in 1960. Pictured are, from left to right, Martha Knowlton, Jack Beals, Eunice Vorys, Howard Tharp, Ina Rostofer Harrison, Thelma Cochenour Cottrell, Howard Hackman, and Helen McDaniel Weaver.

Carol Taylor was crowned homecoming queen in 1961 during halftime of the game between Pickerington and Millersport. The homecoming court includes, from left to right, Sandy Strome, Carolyn Eilbert, Taylor, Sandy Blake, and Vickie Wooley.

This school was on the south side of Route 204, midway between Milnor and Harmon Roads near the DeWitt Clinton Millar home. The schoolhouse also was used for Sunday school services. In 1860, it was listed on the Pickerington circuit of the Methodist church. At that time, the Pickerington circuit included seven churches and eight Sunday schools—the Oak School was the lone Sunday school that was not a church.

Seen here in 1983 at the class of 1923's 60th reunion are, from left to right, (seated) Bessie Diley Evans and Helen Fenstermaker Spears; (standing) Edward F. Brooke, Mary Kraner Biddle, Evelyn Smith Brobst, Dr. Kenneth W. Taylor, and Ruth Taylor Turley.

This 1984–1985 Pickerington High School girls' basketball team won the first of six state championships at the school. Pictured are, from left to right, (first row) Angie Adrean, Tonia Heren, Jayneen Feyko, Janice Franks, Sarah Cloud, and Laura Myers; (second row) Keith Ebright (coach), Lori Sunderland, April Blevins, Laura Wood, Dee Dee Martin, Cindy Hartsell, Karen Blades, Nicole Sanchez, and David Butcher (coach).

In 1849, Robert W. and Susan Bowen gave land for a school at the junction of Bowen and Schoolhouse Roads, on the west boundary of Violet Township. The original land deeded measured only 40 feet square (1,600 square feet) and sold for $1. Additional land was added by Irvin and Florence Bowen in 1898. The schoolhouse still stands today and is used as a residence.

The Oregon School was built in 1865 on Johnston Road (now Pickerington Road) between Stemen and Refugee Roads. John Bowers purchased the land for the school for $5. The building was torn down after consolidation of district schools.

The Allen School stood near where the covered bridge once crossed Blacklick Creek on Tussing Road, just west of Route 256. In 1857, Andrew French and his wife, Francis, gave the land to the Violet Township Board of Education. In 1874, they added additional land to the grant.

Five
RELIGIOUS FREEDOM

Many of the ancestors of Pickerington's first residents came to America because of religious intolerance in their home countries. They wanted a land where they could practice their beliefs without fear of persecution, and Pickerington offered these families a place where they could express their religious freedom.

Pickerington's religious history includes many different congregations, several of which still exist today and some whose names have changed. Each has its own story of origin and survival, as some churches have had to endure heartbreaking incidents. Violet Chapel, for instance, burned down in the 1930s after a bird reportedly carried a lit cigarette into a bird's nest in the bell tower. Members of that congregation split, joining with at least three other congregations at the time.

Other churches have remained and expanded over the years, building additions and new churches as their congregations have grown. By 1990, for example, Seton Parish had grown to include more than 1,000 families. The church responded by constructing a new, larger worship space and opening an activity center.

Though unable to highlight every church and congregation, this chapter shows a common thread among the various denominations. Although some churches have disappeared over the years and others have flourished, all were welcome additions to the community at one time in Pickerington's past.

The first Job's Evangelical Lutheran Church was built in 1833 and named after Job Ziegler, who donated the church site, on Amanda-Northern Road just south of Busey Road. It was one of the first two dedicated churches in Violet Township, built by combined Lutheran and German Reformed congregations who alternated Sundays. This photograph shows the church, rebuilt in 1849, with a new bell tower added in 1902. Although the church is gone, an engraved cornerstone sits in Job's Cemetery.

Established in 1820, the Trinity Episcopal United Brethren Church held services in members' homes until 1848, when the first church building was constructed by members from logs provided by Jacob Good. The structure seen here was completed in 1866 and replaced the old log church. Home now to Resurrection Ministries for All People, this building still exists on the southwest corner of Toll Gate Road and State Route 204.

Dovel Memorial United Brethren Church was built in 1882 at 170 East Columbus Street, adjacent to the Violet Cemetery. The church still stands today, though it is now Unity East Church.

Violet Chapel was built in 1884 at 7475 Refugee Road. The church burned to the ground in the 1930s, reportedly because a bird carried a lit cigarette butt into a bird's nest in the bell tower. After the fire, Violet Chapel members joined three other existing congregations—Trinity United Brethren, Dovel Memorial United Brethren, and the Methodist Episcopal church in Pickerington.

This image, from between 1895 and 1900, shows participants in a Pickerington Methodist Church program. Historians believe it was the "School Days" program, though it may have been a mock wedding. The photograph was likely taken in front of a log house that stood at what is now 155 East Columbus Street, directly across the street from the old Dovel Memorial United Brethren Church.

This program is from the "Memories of the Heroes of Our County" event held on February 22, 1899. Put on by the Ladies' Aid Society of Pickerington Methodist Church, the program featured songs and tableaux—scenes or vivid depictions of events. Presenters included Grace Bowen, Allen Courtright, and James Clem Kraner.

This image shows the last Sunday school service at Pickerington Methodist Episcopal Church before it was razed to build the third and current church on the site. This building was constructed in 1883, and the photograph was taken in 1950. The first church lot was purchased in 1833 from Abraham and Anna Pickering for $2. After the congregation outgrew the first small church, the one seen here was built.

In 1851, this building, at 77 West Church Street, was the first Pickerington Methodist Church parsonage. Since being sold by the church, it has been used as both a residence and a business.

In 1951, the cornerstone for the new Pickerington Methodist Episcopal Church was laid at the corner of Church and Cross Streets. From left to right are Noel Cramer, trustee; Nelson Davis, contractor; Dr. George Wilson, district superintendent; and Stanley Benton, pastor.

Finished in 1952, the Pickerington Methodist Episcopal Church still stands on Cross Street. During construction, services were held in the basement of the Carnegie library. The new church cost approximately $100,000 to finish. The Methodist congregation outgrew this building in 1997 and constructed a new church on the southwest corner of Diley and Long Roads in 1999.

The Epiphany Lutheran Church is located at 268 Hill Road North. This first building was completed in 1962, followed by a large addition dedicated on May 27, 1984. The church continues to serve the Pickerington population, and celebrated its 50th anniversary in 2011.

Father Edward Fairchild officially organized the St. Elizabeth Ann Seton Parish on July 1, 1978, although the Columbus diocese had purchased the 18-acre tract of land in the mid-1960s. Mass and religious education classes were held at Pickerington Middle School until February 1981, when the new church was dedicated at 600 Hill Road North.

By 1990, Seton Parish had grown to include more than 1,000 families, so the church decided to add a new, larger worship space and more classrooms. A new sanctuary was completed, and in 2001, a new activity center opened, offering a full gym, a stage, and a kitchen.

The Holy Redeemer Lutheran Church is under construction in the background of this photograph. The church, built in 1985, was sold in 2007 and currently sits vacant. There is a popular community sledding hill behind the church, near the corner of Route 256 and Route 204. Pisgah Cemetery, in the foreground, was established in 1852 by parishioners of the Pisgah Church, which once stood next to it. Today, the City of Pickerington maintains the grounds.

Six
CLUBS AND ORGANIZATIONS

Clubs and organizations are the heart of every community. They are often made up of volunteers who give their time for the love of the activity or to help others—or sometimes both. Pickerington's history is rich with civic groups that have reached out to fellow citizens in their times of need as well as organizations that have celebrated community activities.

The legacies these groups have left are evident in today's organizations and clubs. Many groups, such as the Lions Club and Melrose Rebekah Lodge, still have the same goal of helping those in need, but have adapted to changing times and changing needs. Other clubs, such as the Independent Order of Odd Fellows (IOOF) band, no longer exist locally. However, the impact the IOOF had on music education and entertainment in the community has resonated through the decades, and its remnants can still be seen today in community concerts and school performances.

Pickerington is known for its band history, but the Pickerington Male Chorus also made a splash. Although the chorus was shorter-lived than many bands, it was much larger, consisting of 35 to 40 men singing together primarily for the joy of singing. The chorus sometimes performed concerts in neighboring communities as well. Eura L. Tussing, who had formal music training, helped the chorus with its performances.

In 1909, a band formed at the Independent Order of Odd Fellows lodge. It was usually comprised of 16 men, all of whom were members of the lodge. Up until 1926, when it disbanded, it was very active and popular in the community, performing several Saturday night concerts every summer. In 1911, a bandstand was constructed on the main square for concerts.

Each year for the homecoming celebration on Labor Day, the Independent Order of Odd Fellows band greeted the 8:30 a.m. passenger train that arrived in town with visitors. Band members would meet in front of the Central House hotel, at 27 West Columbus Street, and would march to the depot to await the train from Columbus. As the train pulled in, the band would play "Home Sweet Home."

One of the highlights of Pickerington's Labor Day parade was the performance by the Odd Fellows' band. There was usually an afternoon program and an evening concert. In addition to Labor Day, the organization was active in Memorial Day celebrations and was in demand for other town activities as well, such as church socials and other holidays.

The Women's Christian Temperance Union (WCTU) was created by women who were concerned about the destructive power of alcohol. Throughout the United States, WCTU groups met in churches to pray and then marched to local saloons where they asked bar owners to close their businesses. Still going today, the group claims to be the oldest continuous nonsectarian women's organization in the world. Members of the Pickerington WCTU in this late-1800s photograph include, from left to right (first row) Jennie Stemen, Catherine Fishbaugh, Sarah Shoemaker, Catherine Miller, Jessie Ricketts, Lindora Taylor, and Mary Bish; (second row) C.J. Brill, Mary Beals, Jemima Taylor, Edna Curtis, Julie Stoner, Martha Moore, Mary Harmon, Rebecca Alexander, and Saphronia Clippinger; (third row) Mary Harris, Lizzie Kraner, Nettie Handshey, Ella Arthur, Abigail Sharpe, Caroline Schultz, Catherine Robinson, and Emma Courtright.

The Violet Grange was organized in 1914 with 35 charter members and has been an important organization in Pickerington's history. Throughout its years, the service organization has adapted to meet the needs of the community. In its earlier days, it planted crops for ill farmers and supplied food and clothing to families who lost their homes in fires. More recently, in 1995, it organized a campaign to raise funds for Christmas decorations in Olde Pickerington Village. Members are seen here in the 1949 Labor Day Homecoming Parade.

Music has always played an important part in Pickerington and Violet Township's history, and in 1951, the community looked forward to watching the brass quartet at Pickerington High School. The quarter that year includes, from left to right, Ed Eakin, Virgil Howdyshell, Roger Burnard, and Kenneth "Skip" Taylor.

This photograph of a 1901 Pickerington baseball team was taken just east of Frank Dovel's residence at 50 Hill Road South. The team photograph includes, from left to right, (first row) George Price, Boyd Dovel, Cliff Moore (mascot), Gus "Stoney" Sallee, and Omar Fenstermaker; (second row) Charles Scott, Charles Arthur (manager), James G. Kraner, Philip B. Mason, C. Frank Shoemaker, and Thomas Kraner. The name Union on the uniforms has no relationship to Pickerington. Player James Kraner worked at the Union store in downtown Columbus and also played on its company team. When the company's baseball team disbanded, Kraner asked for its old uniforms, bringing them home for his Pickerington team to wear.

To this day, the Lions Club's annual Labor Day fish fry is one of the most popular events in the community. The Pickerington Lions Club was chartered on October 24, 1946, with the Canal Winchester Lions Club as a sponsor. The first roster had 38 members. Through its years, it has contributed to the schools, the senior citizens' center, Boy Scout Troop 256, and several other organizations. One of its most popular projects is contributing to sight-saving programs by paying for the cost of eye examinations and glasses for those in need in the community. The Labor Day fish fry is one of the group's main fundraising activities.

Melrose Rebekah Lodge No. 571 was instituted on June 24, 1903. The first meetings were held in the Independent Order of Odd Fellows lodge on the north side of Columbus Street. Through the years, the Rebekah lodge's meeting place has moved several times. The several dozen members in the group today take an active role in helping community members and organizations. In 1969, the members are, from left to right, (first row) Ruth Shields, Narcia Minor, Dorothy Steiger, Helen Spears, and Florence Ford; (second row) Bessie Walton, Mary Weller, Dorothy Brobst, Leona McDaniel, Orda Mauger, and Lucille Poth.

Pickerington Methodist Episcopal Church Class No. 7, comprised of many 1907 community leaders, is shown here. Pictured are, from left to right, (front row) W.W. Milnor, Alpheus Schultz, Simeon Handshey, Abner Goff Harmon, W.H. Kraner, and teacher Thomas Claybaugh; (back row) Samuel Milnor, Lafayette Harmon, J.T. Fishbaugh, Milton E. Taylor, and Jacob Taylor.

Seven
GROWTH AND GOVERNMENT

Violet Township has become the fastest-growing area in Fairfield County. Pickerington stood as a village for more than 100 years before it became a city in 1991. In 1968, the village saw a population boom after the construction of Interstate 70 and the interchange with Route 256, Pickerington's main thoroughfare.

Prior to this, Pickerington and Violet Township's growth was steady, with perhaps the biggest spurt of growth after the railroad came to town in 1880. The railroad laid a path for new markets and industries to move into town. With new businesses came people, and villagers saw their surroundings slowly begin to change.

Between 1905 and 1925, telephone, gas, and electric services came to Pickerington. In the 1930s and 1950s, the fire department found itself moving into new buildings as it continued to grow, and 1960 brought Pickerington's first police chief. Following the construction of Interstate 70 later that decade, new subdivisions began to pop up and change the landscape of the community. In 1970, the census shows 696 residents lived in Pickerington. Just one decade later, there were 3,851.

When the railroad came to town in 1880, it brought immigrants, development, and a new market for farmers' produce and livestock. The view in this early-1900s photograph looks south on High Street (now Center Street) towards the Pickerington depot. During this time, six passenger trains came through Pickerington each day. After train service ended, the depot closed in 1958.

This 1905 view of Pickerington was taken from the Pickerington School on East Street. By the time of this photograph, telephone poles had been installed and the Pickerington Mill—the smokestack in the upper right corner—was producing flour. The tile mill and creamery were also major, successful businesses in town during this time.

A kerosene streetlamp is seen outside the Shoemaker home, at 22 West Columbus Street, in 1905. Kerosene lamps were replaced when natural gas lines were installed in 1908. In 1925, electricity arrived in town, followed by a municipal water system in 1951 and a wastewater treatment plant in 1970.

Postal service came to Pickerington in 1831, and post offices were operated by business owners until 1967. One of these post office locations was P.B. Mason Meat Market and home, shown here at 21 West Columbus Street. Philip "Phil" Mason was appointed postmaster in 1934 and, upon his death in 1940, was succeeded by his daughter, Cleo Mason Richter, who served until 1967 at this same location. Cleo is pictured in front of the meat market with her mother, Jenny, in this 1921 photograph.

The Pickerington Volunteer Fire Department moved into this building on Center Street in 1938. The building also housed the mayor's and village council offices. In 1941, the fire department acquired this new Ford fire truck, one of the most modern fire trucks available at the time.

In 1955, the Violet Township Fire Department was created and a new firehouse was built at 21 Lockville Road. The department was staffed by volunteers until 1985, when the township hired a full-time fire chief and four firefighters. Today, the Violet Township Fire Department serves Pickerington and Violet Township residents from three stations.

In 1954, to make room for the new fire station, Violet Township officials demolished the original 1883 township house and village jail. Residents passed a bond issue in 1953 to build this larger fire station and purchase another fire truck to serve the whole township.

This view, looking west down East Columbus Street in 1967, was photographed just before a new Pickerington Post Office was built at 51 East Columbus Street. This building was dedicated solely to post office operations. The current, larger post office, located at 520 Hill Road North, serves a large portion of Violet Township.

Pickerington hired its first police chief, Wilford E. Johnston, on June 15, 1960. Under the supervision of the Fairfield County sheriff's office, Johnston worked eight hours a day, six days a week, and was on call after his normal hours. His salary was $4,200 per year. The police department operated out of several sites around Pickerington until 1988, when it moved into the vacated post office building at 51 East Columbus Street. In 2002, the city built a new police headquarters on Refugee Road.

Many local drivers know this road, but few have seen it in its early stages. This photograph shows the eastern portion of Interstate 70 in 1966. By 1968, construction crews had completed the interstate's route through the northern portion of Violet Township. An interchange connected the highway to Route 256, Pickerington's main thoroughfare, providing a gateway to Pickerington. Pickerington had 696 residents in 1970; by 1980, it had 3,851.

This was the view from Route 256 in 1958, before Mingo Estates was built. The large white house in the distance belonged to Rev. G.N. Tussing and was at the corner of Refugee and Harman Roads. Development of Mingo Estates began in the late 1960s. It was the first subdivision built outside of Pickerington village limits.

Roy Huntwork's Mobil Station is seen here in 1949 at the corner of Center and Columbus Streets. From 1950 to 1982, Clarence "Dude" Harrel operated it as a Standard Oil station. It was then acquired by Violet Township to use as a second fire station and housed the trustees' office until its current administrative office was built at 12970 Rustic Drive. The building now houses a Fairfield County Sheriff's substation.

After two remodelings, the former Abraham Pickering homestead located on the banks of Sycamore Creek at 500 Hereford Drive became the Pickerington municipal offices in 1977. The 40 acres of surrounding land purchased in conjunction with the historic home became Sycamore Creek Park. The building was condemned and destroyed in 1992, and village employees moved to a newly constructed municipal building nearby at 100 Lockville Road.

The Taylor covered bridge was built in 1873, possibly by Jonathan Coulson or Jacob R. Brandt, across Sycamore Creek on Tollgate Road, north of Refugee Road, and was 60 feet long and 14 feet wide. It remained standing until December 23, 1983, when it collapsed under the weight of a dump truck hauling 15 tons of gravel.

In 1965, officials install a new siren on the roof of the Violet Township Fire Department's new building at 21 Lockville Road. The siren was sounded to call volunteer firemen to the station when they were needed to respond to a fire. The fire department is tasked with serving both Pickerington and the surrounding township.

Eight
Landmarks and Events

As a community that takes pride in its history, Pickerington has worked to preserve several landmarks, each of which tells a unique story. One of the most interesting is that of the Carnegie library, whose building still stands at 15 East Columbus Street and is home to the Pickerington-Violet Township Historical Society Museum.

In the early 1900s, the Violet Township library was a free library that contained 1,189 books. However, it was located in two small alcoves in the school building. The library's board of trustees wanted a better facility, so members applied for a grant from the Carnegie Library Commission in hopes of getting funding for a new library building. The commission contacted the board of trustees and told them they must work with the Violet Township trustees and the Pickerington village council jointly for the project to move forward and receive the $10,000 grant. There were also a few requirements that had to be met: the township trustees had to collect a one-tenth-mill tax to maintain and operate the library, and the library had to be on public land. For this to occur, township officials had to move the township building to the rear of the lot so they could make room for the new building.

However, residents not in favor of paying the tax and constructing a new library circulated a petition that could be filed as an injunction and stop the library from being built. The person responsible for taking the injunction to the Fairfield County courthouse did not arrive on time to file the petition on the first day it could be submitted to county officials. Therefore, the injunction could not be filed until the following morning. That evening, library supporters moved the township house and began digging the foundation for the new library. The petition could then no longer be filed because construction had officially begun.

Dedicated on Labor Day, 1916, the Pickerington Carnegie library served as the public library until 1993. The building is on the southwest corner of Columbus Street and Lockville Road and now houses the Pickerington-Violet Township Historical Museum.

On Pickerington Road just south of Pickerington, the Tabernacle is currently owned by the McGill family. The United Brethren Association signed a 10-year lease in 1889 for land on Pickerington Road owned by Sam Zeigler to hold religious meetings during the summer months. The congregation set up a campground and built a tabernacle using timber from woods on the property, known as Zeigler's Grove.

The Central House hotel, at 27 West Columbus Street, was one of 37 buildings in Pickerington in 1866. The hotel had five upstairs guest rooms and welcomed travelers visiting the village. Mary Snoke, a widow, purchased the hotel from John Moore in 1906 and operated it until she died in 1932. The hotel closed in 1938 and was converted into apartments.

> You and your friends are cordially invited to attend the first annual Home-Coming, to be held at Pickerington, O.,
>
> ## Monday, Sept. 4, 1911.
>
> There will be good music and plenty of entertainment. Come early and bring your basket and enjoy the day.
>
> W. B. TAYLOR, President.
>
> JAMES G. KRANER, Secretary.

Community leaders Dr. W.B. Taylor and James G. Kraner organized the first Homecoming Celebration in Pickerington on September 4, 1911. This turned into an annual event until interrupted by World War II. The well-attended annual homecoming included food, music, a parade, speeches, and sporting games.

This Dovel family home still stands at 380 West Columbus Street in Pickerington. It is also known as the Dovel Bowers House, and is listed in the National Register of Historic Places. The house was originally built for Lucinda Dovel and her husband, Charles Bowers. The home has an eight-sided cupola and a three-room summer kitchen on the north side, disconnected from the house.

This home at 50 Hill Road South was built by Frank Dovel's father, Jacob, and was first occupied by Frank and his family in 1881. Construction of the home took two years to complete. The house, which has 13-foot ceilings, contains 180,000 handmade bricks.

William Smith originally acquired 211 acres, which bordered Routes 256 and 204, in 1866. He and his family lived in this home. In 1935, Columbus Auto Parts owner Reynold Klages purchased the home and acreage and named it Hunter's Run Farm. The Smith home was used as his farm manager's residence. Today, the home serves as the office for Turnberry Apartments on Hill Road.

The 211 acres purchased by Reynold Klages in 1935 now encompass the Hunter's Run, Turnberry, and Cross Creeks shopping centers. On the current Cross Creeks portion of the land, Klages built a spectacular 6,000-square-foot country retreat called the Manor House (pictured) that he used primarily for entertaining. The retreat included a swimming pool, trap-shooting range, winding trails, campsites, lighted tennis courts, and a male-only clubhouse.

The Hunter's Run Farm barn was also known as the Mayflower Barn after it was purchased by A.J. Good of the Pickerington Creamery, the makers of Mayflower Butter. The barn burned down on February 14, 1998. Arson was the suspected cause.

This home was built by one of the Pickering family members and was transferred to the Hizey family on July 6, 1894. It is most recently known as the Acker home. The old Methodist Episcopal church, built in 1883, sits in the background. The house, at 115 North Center Street, now serves as a law office.

This covered bridge was built in 1905 or 1906, and spanned Sycamore Creek on Busey Road. It was roofed with dark wooden shingles and painted white. In 1986, the bridge was damaged by a truck and the Fairfield County engineer decided to demolish it. A group of local residents, however, raised the money to pay for it to be moved on September 7 of that year to Sycamore Creek Park, where it is now lives safely in the park.

Paul Hansen, president of the Lions Club, and Cleo Richter pose for a photograph at the annual Labor Day celebration in 1978. The Lions Club has hosted the celebration since 1949.

This Dovel family home was built for Florence Ann "Florida" and Irven Bowen. Two Dovel sisters—Florida and Olive—married Bowen brothers Irven and Oliver, respectively, in a double wedding on September 12, 1877. This house was built around that time on the southwest corner of Refugee Road and Route 256. The home was razed in 1989 to make room for a new McDonald's.

This photograph of an Olde Village Pickerington streetlamp was taken in 1979. Until natural gas lines were installed in Pickerington in 1908, a lamplighter was paid $100 annually to light the kerosene streetlamps each evening and keep them in good shape. This streetlamp is currently on display at the Pickerington–Violet Township Historical Society Museum.

Here, a young Betty Jane Moore stands with the "Our Boys in the Service" sign in 1943. The sign lists the names of local soldiers serving in World War II. Names were added to the sign as new recruits left home to assist in the war effort. When a soldier was killed in action, a star was added beside his name.

Kerr Mound, on Route 256 east of downtown Pickerington, is an archeological site owned by the city. The property was donated to the city in 1982 after it was looted by archeological hobbyists. The offenders were caught and arrested. It is suspected that the Adena people, a pre-Columbian Native American culture that existed from around 1000 to 200 BC, created the mound.

In 1901, attorney C.O. Beals acquired this home at 5 West Columbus Street. He topped the stone wall seen in this 1950 photo with concrete globe ornaments. Old glass globes from gas streetlights were used as molds. They were filled with concrete so that when the concrete hardened, the glass would break, leaving the shape of the globes.

Kelley's Food Center is seen here in the old Harry Hanna's Auto Dealership building at 30 West Columbus Street. Before Dick and Betty Kelley bought the store, it was known as the Village Food Center. Dick was in the grocery business for 22 years before purchasing his own grocery. In the cold winter months, his wife delivered groceries to many citizens in town. The store was in business through the 1970s.

The Patriotic League participated in the 1918 Homecoming Parade. The pony cart seen here belonged to Evelyn Fishpaw, who married Raymond Boyer. The Patriotic League was a group of local Methodist women who supported prohibition. Just a few months after this photograph was taken, the United States ratified the 18th Amendment, which prohibited the manufacture, sale, or transportation of intoxicating liquors.

Homecoming queen Elizabeth England is seen here with driver Danny Fishbaugh in the 1920 Homecoming Parade. Pickerington homecoming celebrations began in 1911, but parades did not start until 1913.

C.S. Good Garage participated in the 1928 Homecoming Parade, as did several businesses and people in Pickerington and Violet Township. The parade was an opportunity for villagers to come together and celebrate Labor Day and homecoming each year. Just as they do today, parades in the early 1900s included cars, floats, and crowds lining the streets.

Ray Judy, the owner of the Pickerington Greenhouse, entered this float in the 1913 homecoming parade. Judy lived with his wife, Mary, and their daughter, Iva Marie, in this house at 93 West Columbus Street, which was built before 1900. The greenhouse was to the left of the home.

Nine
ARTS AND PEOPLE

From Civil War veterans to famous musicians, Pickerington and Violet Township have an impressive list of successful natives and residents who have left their marks on the community. One of the most notable residents was Eura L. Tussing, who was passionately involved in music and passed his love for it along to his students and the community as a whole. A composer, Tussing wrote several songs that are still sung in churches today.

Local boy Earl Moore pitched for the Cleveland baseball team, now known as the Indians, from 1901 to 1907. He is known for pitching the first no-hitter in the American League—a perfect nine innings. Unfortunately, after he left the scoreless game, a relief pitcher allowed four runs in the 10th inning and Cleveland lost the game.

Violet Township history also boasts a prizefighter, James Jeffries, who became the heavyweight boxing champion in 1899; a concert violinist, John Newman Hizey, who has played for European royalty; and a Miss Ohio, Roxi Erwin, who went on to compete for Miss USA.

Several other people highlighted in this chapter, while not as famous, were important to the history of Pickerington.

Pickerington native John Henry Shoemaker served in the Civil War. He is seen here in his uniform, holding the gun he used while fighting. He went to war as a substitute for Abner Goff Harmon. When he came home, he founded Shoemaker Hardware Store and married Sarah Knepper. He died on July 27, 1907, and is buried in Violet Cemetery.

Two Civil War veterans, Thomas Claybaugh (rear seat, left) and Billy Hoy (rear seat, center), ride in a parade to Violet Cemetery to decorate the graves of Pickerington's fighting men. Both veterans made a profound impression on residents. Hoy served in the cavalry under the command of Gen. Philip H. Sheridan and fought in the famous Battle Above the Clouds at Lookout Mountain, Tennessee. Others in the image are Darius Mosier (front seat passenger), Earl Myers (driver), Ruth Moore (behind car, left), Jeannie Marie Myers (behind car, right) and Gertrude Moore (foreground).

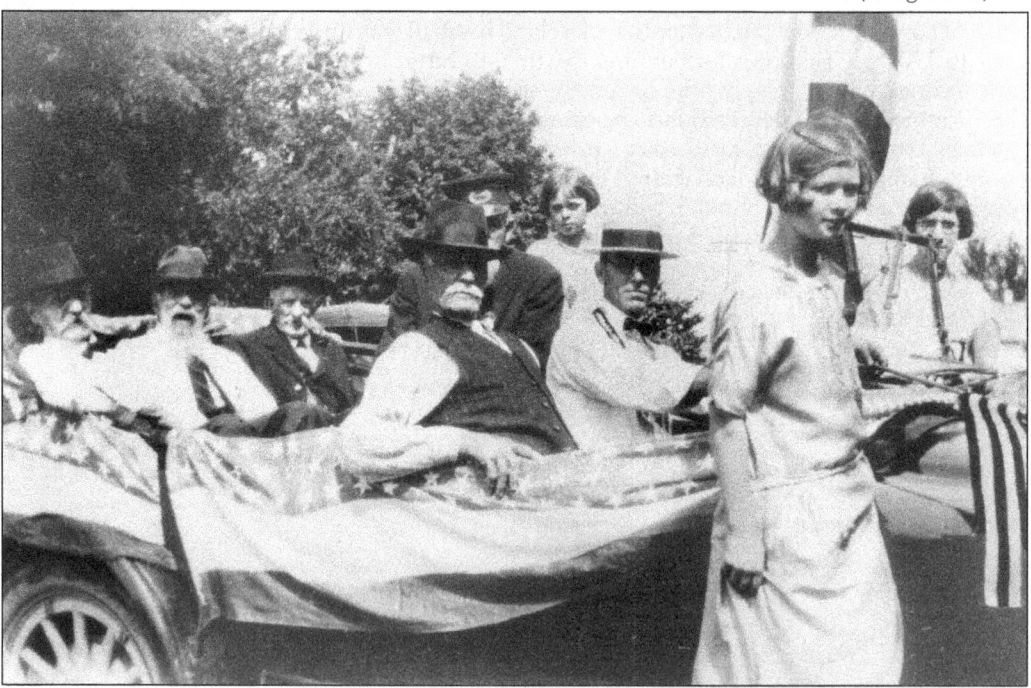

Born in 1871, Eura L. Tussing spent his entire life in the Pickerington area and was the pupil of opera tenor Cecil Fanning. He attended Capitol School of Oratory and Music in Columbus. On the Sunday night before the second community homecoming celebration in 1912, he directed a 70-voice choir in the introductory presentation of his oratorio *Emmanuel*. He died in 1953. As a composer, Tussing wrote several anthems, including "The Star of Bethlehem." Publishing companies printed many of his works, including "My Dearest Friend" (below). Tussing also directed several musical organizations in the Pickerington area, including the Pickerington Male Chorus and the Methodist church choir.

Pass No. 111 for the Cleveland Baseball Company's 1925 season (above) belonged to Earl and Blanche Moore. Moore pitched for Cleveland from 1901 to 1907, and pitched the first nine-inning no-hitter in the American League, on May 9, 1901. Unfortunately, a relief pitcher allowed four runs in the 10th inning and Cleveland lost to Chicago 4-2.

Alonzo Earl Moore was born in Pickerington on July 29, 1877. He was one of 14 children and was noticed by professional baseball scouts while pitching for a semiprofessional team at Bushnel Park in Columbus. In his 14-year major-league career, he won 163 games, lost 154, and had a .141 batting average. Moore and his wife, Blanche, retired to Pickerington. He died on November 28, 1961.

When James Jeffries was eight years old, his family left Violet Township and settled south of Los Angeles. At 17, he went to work in a boiler factory and took up boxing, earning the name "Boilermaker Jim." At 25 years old and 250 pounds, he grew as a prizefighter and became the heavyweight-boxing champion in a match held in 1899 in Coney Island, New York. His boxing days eventually ended, but he continued working with youth and charity programs.

Concert violinist John Newman Hizey was born in 1876 in Violet Township. He went abroad in 1895 and spent five years in Germany studying violin. He was a member of the Gerwandhaus Orchestra and played for European royalty. Hizey returned to the United States and taught string instruments at Ohio University's School of Music. He returned to Pickerington in 1924 and operated a fruit farm on Route 204. He died in 1951 and is buried in Violet Cemetery.

Roxi Erwin represented Fairfield County in the 1984 Miss Ohio USA pageant. She was crowned winner and went on to compete for Miss USA. She is seen here with Pickerington mayor Robert Thomas. Erwin was a podiatric assistant during the time of the competition.

May Dovel, standing in front of the Frank Dovel house at 50 Hill Road South, is dressed in black vintage attire during a 1965 Pickerington Sesquicentennial tour of homes. The other women, from left to right, are Ruth Ann Phillips, Esther Burnham, and Frances Brooke. May and Rose Dovel, daughters of Frank Dovel, inherited the home and 160 acres. Later, the land was divided and sold. Portions of it are home to the city's sewage plant as well as Pickerington High School Central's athletic stadium and Ridgeview Junior High School, located just south of the old Dovel house. The home was restored by Dovel descendent Richard Ricketts and currently houses his law office.

Born in Pickaway County on February 24, 1878, Dr. Georgia Finley graduated from Ohio Medical University in 1898. First licensed in Vinton County, she ran her practice in Pickerington for nine years, from 1902 to 1911, in the house at 8 East Columbus Street. She became the first president of the Violet Township Board of Library Trustees and helped bring a Carnegie library to Pickerington. Finley moved to Gloucester, Massachusetts, in 1911 to do institutional work. She died on April 19, 1915, in Cincinnati. Her funeral was held in Pickerington and she was buried in Nelsonville, Ohio.

Pickerington Village teenagers, from left to right, Evelyn Price, Tarita Shoemaker, and Wyland Houser enjoy a late-March day in front of Shoemaker Hardware at 24 West Columbus Street in 1923. Tarita's parents, C. Frank and Grace, and her grandfather John Henry Shoemaker served area residents with Shoemaker Hardware from 1886 to 1969. All three generations of the Shoemaker family lived next door at 22 West Columbus Street. Note the connecting bridge they constructed between their home and business.

Mingo Estates promoters Roy Huntwork (left) and local veterinarian Dr. S. "Louie" Saylor, are pictured. Mingo Estates was one of the first subdivisions built in Violet Township. The southeast corner of Hill and Refugee Roads was later developed as a shopping area with a water tower, and the homes were located behind. The first section built included 31 homes on Brookside Drive, bordering the south side of the creek. It is commonly called Old Mingo today. The property was originally farmland owned by Henry Taylor, who sold it to Huntwork and Saylor.

C. Frank Shoemaker (left) and Otto Ebright are seen here in 1958 in front of Shoemaker Hardware, at 24 West Columbus Street. Shoemaker inherited the business from his father, John, in 1913. Ebright also served as mayor of Pickerington from 1930 to 1951.

Visit us at
arcadiapublishing.com